Poems to Enjoy

by

Jim McCurry

Jim McCurry

To Chris

DORRANCE PUBLISHING CO., INC.
PITTSBURGH, PENNSYLVANIA 15222

Dorrance Publishing Co., Inc.
701 Smithfield Street
Pittsburgh, PA 15222
Visit our website at *www.dorrancebookstore.com*

ISBN: 978-1-4349-1152-0
eISBN: 978-1-4349-3861-9

ACKNOWLEDGMENTS

I've had lots of encouragement and support putting this selection of poems together.

Many thanks to John Young for his wonderful sketches.

Many thanks and appreciation to Pam McCurry, Mary Jackson, Sue Wright, Nancy Ryder and Joyce McCurry for helping with the selection.

I want to thank Thelma Aparicio for the many hours spent in interpreting, typing and retyping my scribbles from napkins, envelopes, paper sacks, and many other kind of paper – some forty to fifty years old.

A Collection of Poems

Selected from a collection written between 1947 and 2010

By Jim McCurry

Dedicated to my wife, Gail

I'll go there again someday
Among the memories I've hidden away.

Jim McCurry
To
G. M.

Preface

This is the age of the internet, of lightning-speed communications. Cloud computing is coming fast, and it has nothing to do with rain. Where, then, is the need for poetry?

There are souls filled with problems, solutions hard to find, all searching for some form of release, some escape from troubled times.

What's better than poetry, just a few simple words. Words that can move your soul, take you away to another place, another time. If, just for a moment, you can smell the fragrance, see the beauty, and feel the peace of mind, then poetry is needed.

I hope you enjoy these poems. Perhaps they will bring back memories...

> Your first love,
> The first stream you waded,
> The first time you planted flowers,
> The first sound you heard from a turtledove.

Jim McCurry

Contents

World of Poetry

Come walk with me
Into this land of poetry

We'll travel over hills and valleys
Through space and time
While we let our mind
And soul
Enjoy the flow
Of the rhythm and rhyme

Memories

I'll go there again someday
Among the memories I've hidden away;
I'll stroll the places I used to play
And cherish the thoughts in a childish way.

I'll cross the road of youth and joy
To live once more a barefooted boy;
I'll pick a star from heaven's sky
Dream of riches—might even cry.

I'll gather the tears, perhaps to drop again
Reminisce a love, remember a friend;
I'll pause a moment at close of day
To watch the sun as it fades away.

I'll cross the stream I used to wade
Toss a stone to watch the shadow fade;
I'll pick a rose for my mother dear
And imagine things from the sounds I hear.

Yes—I'll go there again someday
Among the memories I've hidden away.

The Meadow across the Brook

I gathered these flowers for you—I picked them from the field
In the meadow across the brook
The one you visited on the day
I had stopped to look.
I thought they might
Brighten your day
And freshen the air
Wherever you stay.

-

I have this picture for you—I took it of the trees
In the meadow across the brook
The one you visit every autumn when you have time
To rest, gaze or just read a book.
I thought you might enjoy the
Colors of your secret hiding place
When winter's cold and
Snow leaves little time to trace.

-

I built a fire for you—I did it with the wood I gathered
In the meadow across the brook
The footprints in the snow
Left little doubt the trail you took.
I thought you might find joy
On this cold winter night
With the warmth from the
Meadow in the fire's golden light.

Reflection

Who is that person in
The mirror I see?
Does he live in
This body with me?
—No—
I may have friends
That look as old as he
But I'm just a boy
That—I'm sure you can see.

A Prayer of Thanks

Thanks for the thorns along the roadside
Thanks for the fireflies to help see by
Thanks for the rain on some cloudy day
And thanks for the sun that helps along life's way.

Thanks for the birds that sing their song
Thanks for the memories of times now gone
Thanks for the snow on some cold day
And thanks for the friends we cherish along life's way
Amen.

Comfort

Don't talk; just let me hold
Your hand and go to sleep.

Those words from my soul mate
Are beautiful memories to keep.

While side by side we sleep

Oak Tree

I should like to climb that tree
Climb to the top
I'd like to feel the cool breeze
And see the sky before I stop.
-

Oak trees are easy to climb
Their limbs grow that way
Nature had little boys in mind
When she made them that day.
-

I would like not to stop
Until I had conquered the last limb
Then catching my breath
Listen to the wind hum a soft hymn.
-

I would like not
To climb back down
But stay with the wind
High above the ground.
-

To see afar
The dream of a boy
On a distant star.

Homeless Man

Where are you going?—To the old man I asked
I'm on my way—to me he replied.

He didn't know where he was going
And if he did he wouldn't tell.

———

Would you like a ride?

———

Where are you going?—to me he asked.
I'm on my way—to him I replied.

I knew where I was going
But I didn't tell.

———

To the old man I lied.

Road Map

Build your castle
In the sky
But plan it well
And build it high.

At the top
Place your heart
Then with faith the task
You can start.

Oh Brother of Mine

Do you remember a place we used to go
After the sun set and the moon came out to glow?

Beyond the barn and down the trail
With me behind so young and frail
Cross the pasture and down to the wood
Occasionally stopping but there we stood.

Oh brother of mine just me and you
I can hear the Whippoorwill, can you too?
Into the woods we followed the trail
Though we are old now, I remember well.

Oh brother of mine

A Game Called Keeps

Once upon a time
In a faraway land
Lived a boy among boys
Who drew circles in the sand.

Under an old oak tree
With shade from the sun
They played a game called keeps
It was thought they played for fun.

A taw I recall
Was the winner's pride and joy
And a pocket filled with marbles
Made a very happy boy.

The marbles made of glass were
More precious than money
And the game they called keeps
Was serious, not funny.

A Gift of Love

I placed a leaf from the tree
In the brook for my love to see
To see how fast it moved from me.

I took a pebble from the sand
Rinsed it clean with my hand.

I took a twig from the tree
Shaped a band for my love to see
To see how beautiful the stone would be.

The stone from the sand
I placed in her hand.

Luis Alejandro

Advice to My Godchild

You came into this world as a little baby boy
healthy, energetic, spreading lots and lots of joy
soon you will be a young boy learning to be a young man.
Enjoy these years of growing; enjoy every day if you can.

(**Now for the advice**)
Time, Health, and Faith are the most valuable things you have.
Time is fleeting, it can't be controlled - use it wisely.
Health requires work and luck. The body is a miracle.
Do everything possible to take care of it.
(this can reward you with some extra time).
Faith will allow you to accomplish anything in life you want to do.
You must have
faith in yourself; faith with work will move mountains.
All things are possible if you believe.

(**Now for the end**)
To be truly happy you must share your rewards with the less
fortunate.

Behold the Beauty

At the close of day
When work is done
Behold the beauty of
The setting sun.

As darkness covers
The fading light
Behold the beauty of
The stars at night.

With the break of dawn
To lighten your way
Behold the beauty of
Another day.

Bud

He left today
To go away
To fight a war
We know not who made

But I hope and pray
Our enemy too
Is fighting as us
For a home and food

Puzzle

There was this puzzle, a long, long time ago
In my life about things
I did not know

I did not know the future and how life might unfold
The path I would travel and the effect that could have
On other lives untold

The action of those that were influenced by me
How that could leave a print on someone
I did not see

In the scheme of life I am forever amazed
The influence one person has on others
While traveling through this maze

If we could unravel the life of one single person
Or remove from this world his or her very existence
We would be totally shocked how different the world would be
I'm not only thinking about people like Hitler, Einstein or Lincoln
I'm talking about anyone anyplace in this world

This puzzle still exist today
And we need to be more aware
of the things we do or say

Homeless People

To people on the street
To little kids waiting in line to eat
I dedicate my life and promise to keep
A place in my heart for each one I meet

Cycle of Life

Time will do away with
All living things
And with tomorrow's sunrise
Cometh a new day
Rejoice in this day
And mourn not what time has altered.

-

Instead take in your hand
This dust from the good Earth
And let the wind—the restless wind
Return it to its own
To replenish and revitalize
The cycle of life.

Decision

If this should be death
And I chose not to go
Mortal I am
But destiny I hold.
-

I would always be burdened
That I did not know
God's mysterious wonders
And what death doth hold.
-

And so it is
With life today
It's mine to live
And I want it this way.

Dreams Come True

Be a dreamer my friend dream of things to come
And if you are down
Dream when nothing else
Can be found

But dream of greatness and
Things you might do
In life's little triumphs and failures
Dreams will help see you through

Dream my friend of happiness
Whatever you conceive of that to be
Dreams do come true
Come walk in that dream and you will see

Emilie

From France to our home
She came one day
With jeans and t-shirts
And a short time to stay.

Texas our Texas she
Wanted to see
"Boots" we added so
A cowgirl she could be.

I call her—Jolie—though
Emilie is her name
In France I'm sure
They are one and the same.

I listen very carefully when
She talks (I have to)
And I'm fascinated how quick
And precise she walks.

She scored 28
On my Simon game
And now I will not rest
Until I score at least the same.

She tiptoed into our life
For a short time
With jeans and t-shirts
The Marilyn Monroe kind.

Now from Texas she must leave

Jolie—Jolie—I hope you have enjoyed your stay
We have been pleased with your presence
And would like you to come back someday
S'il te plait

Funeral

Oh how sad
To hold back the dead
So people can see
How beautiful a funeral can be.
Yes
Gather ye foe or friend
After my end
Weep, rejoice or mend
But please only pennies you spend
Give my ashes to the wind
And with the keep
Feed the homeless on lonely street.

The Past

Memories linger words spoken often linger
To unusual places a dream untold
Of thoughts forgotten a dream could hold
She was beautiful, old though young
She moved away towards the sun
Yearly she visited older she grew
Time can change beauty too.

Now strange it seems
That stumbling I dream
To cast me thinking to unravel the seam
Fate dropped by to uncover the past
To leave a message my heart to task
To shine tomorrow a lightning glow
Until the truth my heart to know.

On This Day I Thee Wed

Love of my life
First husband—first wife

-

Together we stand
Hand in hand
To repeat these vows
Before God and man

-

Joined at last
Blessed with the past

-

Life with love is
Wonderful, beautiful and sweet
Our love
I pray will keep

The Graveyard

I saw that grave last year when I passed this way
The flowers and little shrubs were green
And I knew they were planted that day.

Mr. Carson it was; he lived in the village nearby
I remember because he died
and no one knew why.

The shrubs and flowers were green and fresh with care
But now such a short time has passed
And they are withered and bare.

I wonder if he is forgotten this soon
And only a year today since I passed this way.

Passing of a Friend

Somewhere between today and yesterday
Memories of our childhood had faded away
Your leaving caught me by surprise
(Although I was told it was not unexpected)
It did bring back to me another day another sunrise.

We were young and at play
We were friends, the world was bright
It seems we were together both day and night
Your presence I still cherish.

Somewhere between today and yesterday
Life has passed away
I have only memories to cling to.

Phrases and Phases No. 1

When I was Four

An old woman once above this very Earth
A mother to a baby she gave birth
From this baby there grew a boy
A boy of youth that knows only joy.

With this boy there lived a dad
And mighty proud of the son he had
To his son he used to say
Jim, you'll follow in my steps someday.

Now Jim's dad was a man of God
A better road will never be trod
There at Concord he used to preach
Even in the wilderness he used to teach.

And of that church many memories I keep
For I was four when he went to sleep
Then by the church they left him one day
With only a mound to show where he lay.

Now Jim's heart was but that of a child
And this parting he thought would be only awhile
So Jim and his mother returned alone
To the little house he called his own.

Phrases and Phases No. 2

Now Seven Years More

I think I should have liked for my dad to say
When from childhood I grew one day
Son I think it's time we talk
So tell your mom we're going for a walk.

As we would have walked that day
His story would start probably this way
Now son from youth you soon must grow
But there are a few things I think you should know.

First of all I'm proud of you son
And I'll always be until my life is done
Maybe I've failed you in a lot of ways
But mostly it was when I forgot to pray.

Now son I've given you all I could
But you are not indebted I want that understood
And son you know there will always be
A welcome here from mom and me.

However I know what my dad would say
When from childhood I grew that day
Son I know you missed me since I went to sleep
—In you I'll live, take care of mom—
This promise you have to keep.

Whatever Has Been—Will Be (Song)

I remember the flowers that bloomed in spring
On fields now covered with snow
I remember a rainbow after the rain
Where now in silence I shiver with cold.

Whatever has been—will be——
My friend
Whatever has been—has been
Whatever has been—will be—
My friend
Whatever has been—has been

I remember the birds that sing their song
In trees now covered with snow
I remember a house I called my own
It was a long, long time ago.

Whatever has been—will be——
My friend
Whatever has been—has been
Whatever has been—will be—
My friend
Whatever has been—has been

I'll Be There (Song)

I'll be there in the morning
I'll be there
I'll be there in the morning
I'll be there

I'll be there in the morning
I'll be there in the morning
I'll be there in the morning
If you wish

I'll be there in the evening
I'll be there
I'll be there in the evening
I'll be there

I'll be there in the evening
I'll be there in the evening
I'll be there in the evening
If you wish

I'll be there for the wedding
I'll be there
I'll be there for the wedding
I'll be there

I'll be there for the wedding
I'll be there for the wedding
I'll be there for the wedding
If you wish

Back to Virginia (Song)

Mary oh Mary I love you
Love you with all my heart
Mary oh Mary I miss you
Miss you since we had to part
-

Come—back to Virginia
Back to the bright starry sky
Whisper you'll love me forever
Forever means never goodbye
-

Virginia oh Virginia is weeping
Weeping since you went away.
Come back—come back my darling
Come back—forever to stay.
-

Come—back to Virginia
Back to the bright starry sky
Whisper you'll love me forever
Forever means never goodbye.
-

Mary oh Mary I miss you
Miss you since you went away
Each minute without you
Grows longer and longer each day
-

Come—back to Virginia
Back to the bright starry sky
Whisper you'll love me forever
Forever means never goodbye.

I'll Be Home (Song)

When autumn turns the leaves to gold again
And the trees above are open wide within
When the snow is falling quiet
On your windowsill at night
Watch for me wait and see
I'll be home.

Yes—I'll be home
When autumn turns the leaves to gold again
I'll be home
When the trees are open wide within
When the snow is falling quiet
On your windowsill at night
Watch for me—wait and see
I'll be home.

Yes I'll be home I'll be home
Watch for me—wait and see
I'll be home
Watch for me—wait and see—I'll be home.

What's It All About (Song)

The rain falls softly as crystal thoughts reach me
A flower blooming, a rainbow unending
That night with you love, was bright like the dawn
But life drew us apart so time could move on.

What's it all about? Am I like the rest?
Why did you have to take the only dream I had
No time for sadness, no reason to cry
My tears won't bring you back
You're gone now, goodbye.

The ground is covered with snow from the sky
A tree is standing, as lonely as I
That day with you love, we walked side by side
But pride pulled us apart, with no place to hide.

What's it all about? Am I like the rest?
Why did you have to take the only dream I had
No time for sadness, no reason to cry
My tears won't bring you back
You're gone now, goodbye.

Those years are gone now, just memories to cling to
They'll always live with me, like I lived with you.
They'll always live with me, like I lived with you.

Soul Mate (Song)

You're my love
My love
The one I'm dreaming of
You're my love
My love
The one I'm thinking of.

You're all I know of heaven
And all I need to love
You're the cutest little starlight
of all the ones above
Your beauty glows like diamonds
it sparkles in your eyes
You are the cutest little starlight
and darling I know why.

You're my love
My love
The one I'm dreaming of
You're my love
My love
The one I'm thinking of
You're my every little heartache
All my dreams come true
You're the maker of perfection and
Darling I love you

Freedom Lives (Song)

Freedom lives—freedom lives
For the young—for the old
Freedom gives—Freedom gives
All the dreams—life can hold.

Come walk with me
Across this great land
Travel the highways and by ways
From the mountains to the sand.

-

Stay with me in the country
Stay with me in town
Visit my brothers—my sisters
Wherever they are found.

-

Listen to their story
Listen to their song
Praise God for freedom
Freedom makes us strong.

-

Freedom lives—freedom lives
For the young—for the old
Freedom gives—freedom gives
All the dreams—life can hold.

-

Freedom lives—freedom lives
For the young—for the old
Freedom gives—freedom gives
All the dreams—life can hold.

I'd Do the Same (Song)

Yes I have been down this road before
I've traveled this and many more
But looking back I wouldn't change
I'd do it all I'd do the same

I've been up
And I've been down
I've seen the world
And all around

I've been rich
And I've been poor
I've been loved
And even more

Yes I have been down this road before
I've traveled this and many more
But looking back I wouldn't change
I'd do it all I'd do the same

I've been good
And I've been bad
I've had fun
And I've been sad

I've been right
And I've been wrong
I've been here
And I've been gone

Yes I have been down this road before
Traveled this and many more
But looking back I wouldn't change
I'd do it all I'd do the same

Yes—looking back
I wouldn't change
I'd do it all
I'd do the same

I'll Be Your Friend (Song)

With a little love, there is a little hate
In every marriage you have to give and take
But every day I'll be your friend
In every way until the end.

Love is a dream, we dare to live
Hand in hand with vows we give
Take this woman; take this man
Seal the dream with a wedding band.

With a little love, there is a little hate
In every marriage you have to give and take
But every day I'll be your friend
In every way until the end.

Bless be the one who's found a friend
Someone to love someone to fend
Live this life side by side
With only love to be their guide.

With a little love, there is a little hate
In every marriage you have to give and take
But every day I'll be your friend
In every way until the end.

Blue Grass Blues (Song)

I wonder why the world is round
I wonder why you turned me down
I wonder why we all must die
I wonder why
I wonder why

I wonder why the good is bad
I wonder why my heart is sad
I wonder why we all must die
I wonder why
I wonder why
I wonder why
I wonder why

Fraulein (Song)

Fraulein, Fraulein I met you one day
On the banks of the old River Rhine
And there we talked while hand and hand we walked
In the sand near the old River Rhine

I remember the day I sailed away
From the bank of that old River Rhine
As the mountains grew small I could barely see at all
Fraulein by the old River Rhine

Fraulein, Fraulein I'll meet you someday
On the banks of the old River Rhine
Once more we'll talk while hand and hand we walk
In the sand near the old River Rhine

Yes—once more we can talk while hand and hand we walk
In the sand near the old River Rhine

The Dreamer (Song)

I was born — a roving cowboy
Born to ride — the open range
With my horse — and my saddle
I'll learn to live — with little change

I know the life — I have traveled
I know the way — to go back
But I'm pleased — to be a rambler
And I'm never — going back

What a pleasure — to see the sunshine
What a gift — to see the stars
What a perfect — world around me
Without the buildings — and the cars

If you want — to join my journey
Come along — as you are
Leave behind — your wealth and worries
And bring along — your old guitar

What a pleasure — to see the sunshine
What a gift — to see the stars
Leave behind — your wealth ad worries
And bring along — your old guitar

Jim McCurry

Quote

Go gracefully into your old age
You have but one way
And maybe one day.

Quote

If you are lucky to have them in your life
The three people that love you the most
Will be your mom, dad, and soul mate.

Quote

We are born—
Then we die—
And in between
We try to figure out why.

Quote

I eat to live, I don't live to eat

Quote

Never hang around in life with people who don't
want to see you succeed.

A Fact

The past is just a moment in time
It could be two hours, two days or infinity.

The past is a fact that cannot change
Except in one's mind
And more often than not
With time this happens.

Kiss

I have a dream from time to time
In secluded places where my love I find
Glass to glass we sip the wine—her hand in mine.

I steal a kiss from time to time
In secluded places where my love I find
Soft, sweet, tender lips—her beauty divine.

The Garden of Flowers

The garden is covered with bountiful flowers, colors of all kind
Forever changing—with the wind and passing of time

Beautiful garden
wonderful flowers
flowing serenity

Someone with the hands of an artist must have labored for hours,
To mold—such a beautiful garden of flowers

Our World

Time is not life
Time has no beginning
And no end
Infinite
Without limits of any kind

Not so with life, all life has
A beginning and an end
A finite amount of time
So too does our world
Protect it
So it doesn't end

Butterfly

Butterfly, butterfly
Spread your wings and fly
The ground is too low
The sky too high

Nectar can be found
Somewhere between the sky and ground

Butterfly, butterfly
Spread your wings and fly
Life is too short
For you and I

Mark and Jeff

Dedicated to My Sons

Son I want you to know
I missed the little boy I used to hold,
I missed his joy, his laughter, his love for life
He created so much happiness and so little strife.

I missed that little boy
I missed him so much
I didn't want to let him go

But he is gone now—forever
Forever from you and from me
Oh I'll not say forever from me
For perhaps he'll visit someday, when I dream

I want you to know that in his place I have a son
And the little boy I loved so much
Would be proud of the adult he has become

Needless to say
I had faith in that little boy
I also have faith in you and your judgement
And I wish you a life filled with happiness and joy

Someday—when you have a little boy or girl
And they journey your way
You'll understand what I'm trying to say.

Rendezvous with Life

See—there—just beyond the creek
There in the stillness, see that's what I tried to keep.

There among the leaves I once found
A dream of fortune no human can tear down
A sweeping stillness my heart desired
Of calm environments that life so mired.
An opening of enchantment with beauty enclosed
A reality of fate but never to impose.

In my passion I searched for a way
To continue that dream forever and ever a day
But as a day to night and a night to day
A child must carry the future his way
So below that tree many autumns ago
I sat reminiscing, a rendezvous I hated so.

Sleep

There is a place I go
—Too often I know—
I go there at night
To visit and revisit before daylight.

Sometimes I sleep until the break of day
What a waste of time to sleep one's life away.

Sour Docks

A warm spring that year had turned the hills and valleys
Around my hometown green
And a cool breeze that day was making
Soon to be summer feel like a wonderful dream.

Maybe I had stopped to sit and watch a grasshopper
Or perhaps to rest and watch the clouds pass by
I don't remember the day, I can't remember the place
And furthermore I don't think it's important that I remember why.

I do remember chewing the sour dock
That's what we called them back then
The fields were covered with sour docks, sour docks everywhere
Oh how I would like to see them again.

Snow at Night

Have you ever waken on a cold winter night
To listen for snow
Silent soft and slow
Falling so quiet?

-

Tiptoeing through the night
Soft slow and white
Turning darkness into light
Peaceful and quiet.

-

On a cold winter night.

The Eagle

The eagle soars
In majestic flight
Golden brown with head, neck
And tail of white.

He spreads his wings
Above the crags so high
Soaring to impossible places
Up in the sky.

Front row: Jace, Cole, Jake, Luke, Beth
Back row: Julie, Jeff, Gail, Jim, Mark, Pam

The Family Portrait

The old camera clicked
And captured a moment in time
Of three generations
A snapshot on paper
To be passed down to future generations.

Some place in time a
Grandmother or granddad
May hold this picture
Talking with their grandchildren
"See the young ones—one is my great—great
Grandmother or granddad
I am not sure which one
The writing on the back has faded with time
The ones in the middle are their moms and dads
And see the two older ones in the back
That's their grandmother and granddad."

One grandchild may ask "where did they live?
What did they do?"

"I don't know
That was a long, long, time ago."

Thoughts of a Teacher

I met thee once just for a moment
In eternity's spacious time
I saw thy beauty thy love
And nature's greatest mind.

I walked with thee and talked
With thee
I even hoped much greater thy
Greatness would be.

Just for a moment I stood in thy presence
With the future of thy greatness in my hand
I stood with thy image oh so humble
Least thy future I ban.

I stood
As any teacher would stand
On the brink of eternity
With the mold of history in my hand.

Tiananmen Square

Yesterday he was alive
Now he's dead
As fresh red blood flows
From the young boy's head.

The blood soaks
His silk black hair
He's only a protestor, a lifeless protestor
After Tiananmen Square.

The Old Shade Tree

The little toys sit under
The old shade tree
I see them almost everyday
It's like they're waiting for me

But I know who they're waiting for
My grandkids
Who played with them
When they were kids

Now they've grown and
Have other places they'd rather be
Places without the toys
And their climbing tree

I know I should give the toys away
Find some place they could stay
With a big shade tree
And some children to play

But maybe the tree like me
Would miss the toys
If I should come home and didn't see
My grandkids and toys

Under the old shade tree

Jim McCurry

The Work of God

When babies are born along life's way
It's nothing unusual
Happens everyday

It's just the work of God
Lending his children for a trial test
To fill a home
A mother's request

When someone dies along life's way
It's nothing unusual
Happens everyday

It's just the work of God
Reclaiming his children that passed the test
To offer them
Eternal rest

Tick Tock

Tick tock— tick tock—goes the clock
Wind it up—wind it up
Before you stop.

Yesterday when I was four
Only time seemed never more.

Yesterday when I was ten
Wishing only I was older then.

Yesterday when time was cheap
Precious time was lost in sleep.

Tick tock—tick tock—goes the clock
Winding down—winding down
Soon will stop.

Time

I stood watching my children play
Thinking about time and how time slips away.
I sat watching my grandchildren play
Thinking about time and how time slips away.
-

I woke up this morning to another birthday
Still thinking about time and how time slips away.
Oh I've tried to stop it, hold it, but it just won't stay.
So I'll keep on thinking about time and how time slips away.

To Kill a Cat

To kill a cat
A destroyer without soul
A murderer, a thief, even hungry and cold
Couldn't kill a cat
A helpless cry
Not eye to eye.

Where Did They Go?

Son, come give Dad a hug I said
While napping on my bed
You were playing on the floor
Like you had so many times before

Before you grew up from being
A little boy.

The Green Silk Gown

The young lady wearing a green silk gown
Stopped at my table
And the casino shut down
You could hear a pin drop
From a hundred feet round
The crowd stood in silence – quiet all around
This beautiful young lady with the coal black hair
Hanging down one shoulder – touching the green silk gown

She took a chip from my stack
A 100 grand chip and slapped it down
She looked at the dealer and said shuffle the deck
He stared into space totally spellbound
Shuffling the cards without looking down
Now deal me the Ace and the queen of town
He dealt the cards
This time looking down

"Is that possible I thought to myself"

Out came the Ace followed by the Queen
Then she tossed back my chip and gathered up her mound
There was a split down the back
Of her green silk gown
But covered everything else
Down to the ground
As she slipped into the crowd I heard her exclaim
I'm out here – I'm homeward bound

Jim McCurry

Watering the Flowers

When the stress of the day
Gets in my way

I water the flowers

The fresh smell
Tells me all is well

While waiting for the spring showers.

You and I

Sometime when I sleep
I dream of days gone by
We are wandering down
An old country road, just you and I.

Hand in hand
We pass the time away
Listening to the birds and bees, wind in the trees
And the sounds they have to say.

Sometime when I sleep
And dream of days gone by
I dream of you, I dream
Of you and I.

The Angels Sing with Joy

Death knocked at her door that day
He only paused momentarily while passing her way
He had called at this door many times before
And remembered the shattered walls and broken down floor.

Only by chance had he stopped this day
He had intended to travel another way
The old lady may be lonely tonight
He'd stop to make sure everything is all right.

He had wanted so many times to take her away
But she insisted on staying—she wanted it that way
Tonight he could feel a void from within
And to his disbelief a voice calling come in.

Could it be true—had she changed her mind
Would she come travel with him? If only her hand he could find
Softly her voice whispered—help me my friend
Release me my children—let me go—let me go with the wind.

Lasting Love

I saw you once at sunrise
Many, many moons ago
And when we met, I knew you would be my sunshine
And I'd never let you go.
-

Since we have walked many beaches at sunset
And held hands in the moonlight
We have spent many happy days together
And I've dreamed by your side every night.
-

I guess I'm just a dreamer
But sometimes dreams come true
Just think after all these years
I'm still in love with you.

Recipe for Sleep

After the long day is finished
And you rest your weary head
Release from your mind
The bad memories before you go to bed.

Keep the good memories
They're fewer in number and easier to recall
I think then, your dreams will be good ones
And sleep will be no trouble at all.

Hitchhiker

I would not have passed
That young person 30 years ago.
For I too once was a hitchhiker
And had done so along this very road.

Hitchhiking was a common way of traveling
Back then
And I seldom ventured far from home
Without waving my thumb in the wind.

I could probably write a book
About the adventures of traveling that way.
The people, places—oh—what stories I could tell
But I'll save them for another day.

Instead—I did not stop
Why? The thought entered my mind.
What has changed?
What has happened, in such a short period of time?

She knows

I have a bond
More closer than kin
With someone I love
Now gone with the wind.
-
But at close of day
When the cool wind blows
It whispers to me
She knows—she knows.

True Love

I have submitted to you
And you have submitted to me
True love
That will live throughout eternity

-

I'll seal this bond we share together
By touching your lips with my hand
Fill the warmth of the sun
On your back from the sand

-

Soft smooth warm sand
Falling softly from my hand
Making a pyramid on your breast
With the sand—from my hand

Ratio of Time to Life

One half score
And two years more
Time is like paste
Life has time to waste

One score
And five years more
Time has no haste
Life has time to waste

Three score
And ten years more
Time has haste
Life has no time to waste

Dream

I dreamed about you last night
We were sitting together talking
You were beautiful.
I think we were somewhere in flight.

I have no idea from where we came
Or to where we were going.
I do remember we were having fun
And you looked just the same.

The same
As that young and beautiful girl
The first time we met
The first time I whispered your name.

A Poem Is Never Finished

The poem on my desk
Will be moved one day
And placed somewhere to rest.

Oh—I'll bring it back someday
Make some changes
Then decide if I should keep or put it away.

To finish on some future day

Spring Time in the Mountains

It's spring time in the mountains
That's my definition of love
The hills and valleys are green
With a beautiful blue sky above

The water is on a mission
Filling the creeks and streams
Rushing to its destination
Making music like a symphony of strings

The pines and aspens are mixed
With many colors of green
And the wind and sun brings life
To this wonderful beautiful scene

Go there in the spring time
You will love what you find
Take with you your soul mate
And leave your worries far behind

A Cottage Small by a River Wall

The cottage small
Stands by a river wall
Listening to the water
Rushing to a rocky waterfall.

Many years ago
What a beautiful sight to see
A small simple cottage
And for someone a home to be.

The river is unstoppable
Time has taken its toll
The cottage now is unlivable
And soon gravity will take hold.

And the river wall
Will no longer hold the cottage small.

Advice to Newlyweds

"Never go to sleep at night
When you are mad at each other
Make up or stay up."

Flowers

Morning time brings day time
Day time brings sunshine
Sunshine grows flowers

I picked this selection for you
I hope they bring you
Many—many happy hours

And when the sun goes to sleep
They're still yours to keep
They're your flowers

Daydreaming

We all daydream, some more than others

When the conscious mind is left free to think
More often than not, daydreaming takes place
We will never know what one dreams
For they would never tell

—

However

—

What if we had to share our dreams
With their dreams and all the world could see
All the dreams we've dreamed
Since we've became you and me

What is Love

Perhaps love is like a turtledove
The dove you seldom see
The voice is always soothing
Like the sounds of the sea

Perhaps love is like a lightning storm
That echoes in your mind
Waiting for the thunder
That follows not far behind

Perhaps love is like a sunset
That colors the distant sky
And the beauty of that sunset
Is like the kindness in your eyes

Perhaps love is like a resting place
Somewhere you want to be
The memories of that place
Will always be of you and me

The memories of love will always be
Memories of you and me

The Old School

The old school
Sits on a hill
Facing the road
From Bettie to Simpsonville

Many kids
Remember the thrill
Of that old school
Called Union Hill

I have many friends
Some now gone
That walked those halls
And the memories live on

I went back
To the old school today
And walked the grounds
Where we used to play

Friends

They're gone now
They been gone for a long, long time
I still miss them
They were good friends of mine
-
Good friends are hard to find

Happy Birthday
To My Soul Mate

I remember the first celebration date
My gift was chocolate pecan candy
And a poem
We set up late—late—late

Your second Birth date
I had to work late
I forgot
That was a big mistake

The third Birthday we had a date
To go to Moon's for a Moon Burger
I had to work late
That was a terrible mistake

On this Birthday I'll make no mistake
I'm sending flowers
For safety's sake
I may have to work late

Sunset

Sunset and evening clouds
Cover the setting sun
Like a paint brush with many colors
Rushing to finish a work undone

You need to watch a sunset
Then you'll regret having missed all the others
For the greatest artist could never create
What nature can do with colors

Poems of Yesteryears

I leave to you my poems
My poems of yesteryears
In them you will find my joy
And you will find my tears

For I too am mortal
And must cross that bridge someday
But I hope when that day has ended
These poems will help the memories stay